People

Skills

Building _Better_ Relationships

Cary Cavitt

Author, Speaker & Founder
Service that Attracts Seminars TM
www.carycavittconsulting.com

Other Authored Books

Service Starts With a Smile

Customer Service Superstars

Five-Star Service

Winning the Customer

Luxury Service

Books may be purchased at:
www.carycavittconsulting.com

Healthy Relationships:

A relationship that consistently brings out the best in each other.

Table of Contents

Introduction

We will always be at our best when we bring out the best in others.
- Cary Cavitt

What is it that allows some people to consistently have healthy relationships while others struggle and always look as if they are caught in a web of unhealthy relationships? Why are some people better in their people skills than others? Is there a secret in learning to build better relationships? These are great questions that we will be addressing in the following pages. My goal is to clearly show that building better relationships and improving on our people skills is a direct result of developing more qualities into our own lives. In other words,

Better people skills and healthier relationships correlate with the number of inner virtues that we have developed in our own lives.

If we are to build better relationships, the first and most important area that we will need to focus on *is ourselves*. It must start with taking an accurate and intimate look into our own lives and count how many virtues that we possess, and how many are missing. When we do this, we will begin to discover that the virtues that are missing *may be the reason that we are not content with the relationships that we have had in the past.*

1

If we are to improve with our people skills, we must understand that the qualities within essentially will determine how we treat others. For instance, if we are impatient with people, we will tend to treat them in a manner that reflects annoyance. On the other hand, if we have developed the virtue of patience, we will find that our treatment toward others immediately improving. Not only will we be more understanding, but we will also be more considerate in our conduct.

Having excellent people skills is nothing more than treating others in a manner that we would like to be treated ourselves. *The healthiest relationships bring out the best in each other because they consistently are showing a large percentage of the virtues that we will be discussing in the following pages.* If we are to improve and become better at building relationships, we must first examine ourselves and learn to develop more of these qualities into our lives.

When all is said and done, most of what will be shared is simple common sense. These virtues are nothing new. As a matter of fact, they have been around for centuries and have worked in every generation. It does not matter what part of the world we may visit or the culture involved, every person will recognize these sixty-five inner qualities as good character traits. *All it takes is to start with one virtue and build from there.* Before long we will find that each new virtue that is gained will begin to enhance not only our relationships, but also our very lives.

✍

May we be to others what we wish others to be to us.

Best regards,
Cary Cavitt

This book is dedicated to those who have shown by their example how to treat others respectfully.

People Skills: pē′pəl skils

Having the ability to bring out the best in another person.

Part I

65 Healthy Qualities

Quality #1

Healthier relationships result when we show …

Acceptance

Acceptance makes others feel welcomed.

Every person has an inner need to feel accepted. This is just part of our human nature. This is one of the reasons that we feel timid when we move out of our comfort zone and enter a situation where we may not know anyone. We feel uncomfortable because of the fear of being rejected or judged. Our defenses are up because we silently wonder if we will be accepted.

We are not alone. The fear of being rejected is universal. With this being the case, *it should make us more aware when we come in contact with a person who may be in a strange situation and does not appear to know anyone. This gives us a perfect opportunity to welcome them and show ourselves to be friendly.* This little gesture will help to ease their uncomfortable feeling of being the stranger in the crowd.

The act of acceptance also does not mean that we always agree with the way a person may choose to live his or her life. But what it does mean is that we accept the person as a human being who has similar feelings like us. When we show a friendly and accepting attitude, we are telling them by our actions that we are not there to judge. This also gives the person a great first impression about us. He or she will remember our kindness in welcoming them.

Lesson...

Showing acceptance conveys that we are non-judgmental.

Quality #2

Healthier relationships result when we show …

Appreciation

Appreciation makes others feel special.

It has been said that one of man's greatest desires is to be appreciated. This is because we feel valued when another person has recognized us. It could be something that we did, or simply an inner quality about us. Appreciation is accepted universally and is a virtue that gives another person a sense of worth.

If we are to become our best, it is essential that we learn to show others that we appreciate them. Maybe it is something they did or said. Maybe it is something about their personality that we find likable. *Whatever it is, the important point is to let others know that we appreciate them.* It can be as informative as expressing a kind word or writing an appreciative letter to the person.

By expressing appreciation, we also are showing others a quality that they may not have recognized in themselves. We are essentially helping this person by recognizing something that can bring out certain gifts that he or she may not have been aware of. Remember to show sincere appreciation and watch your people skills begin to improve considerably.

Lesson...

Expressing appreciation conveys that we recognize a good quality in another person.

Quality #3

Healthier relationships result when we show …

Attentiveness

Attentiveness makes others feel important.

Being attentive in the presence of another person is a positive virtue because of what it conveys. *When we give our full attentiveness, we are in effect telling the person that he or she is important enough to have our undivided attention.* This also lets the person know that we respect what is being said.

Another feature of being attentive is that it makes people feel significant. Comparable to the other virtues, showing attentiveness conveys a sense of importance to the person. By simply giving our full attention, we allow people to express themselves more freely. We are telling them by our attentiveness that they are important.

If we are to show our best by bringing out the best in others, we need to be aware of how we conduct ourselves when we are in a conversation. It is essential to be attentive and give others our full attention. People in turn will appreciate the fact that we have allowed them the opportunity to share.

Lesson...

When we are attentive toward others, we are expressing that we value them.

Quality #4

Healthier relationships result when we show …

Authenticity

Authenticity makes others be more real.

If we are to develop better people skills, we will want to be as authentic as possible. This simply means that we are not trying to appear to be someone else. By being ourselves, we become more comfortable without attempting to be something that we are not. Our authenticity will also allow others the freedom to be more genuine with us.

People appreciate when we are real with them. Nobody likes when another person pretends to be something that he or she is not. To be genuine is comparable to giving the green light for others to be more real with us. It frees them from having to appear to be someone else.

We will always show our best when we stop attempting to be someone else and simply be ourselves. This is because being authentic is the only way to feel comfortable. By not pretending to be someone that we really are not, we will soon discover that we become our best by simply being our real selves. Others will appreciate our authenticity and hopefully make them feel relaxed enough to be more authentic toward us.

Lesson...

When we stop trying to be someone we're not, we will help others to be more authentic as well.

Quality #5

Healthier relationships result when we show …

Benevolence

Benevolence makes others respond favorable.

How we treat others can be said to be a reflection of who we are on the inside. To show benevolence toward another is to show the best in ourselves. Even the most aloof person takes notice when kindness has been displayed. It is a quality that everyone on earth recognizes as a good character trait.

We will always show our best to others when we treat them in a kind manner. This is because every human being appreciates when another person has treated him or her with benevolence. It attracts simply because everyone recognizes this virtue as a sign of charity. Showing our best will always be marked with this behavior.

In order to have healthier relationships, we need to see people as having a desire to be treated with kindness. Having this belief will automatically make our relationships stronger because of the goodwill that a benevolent heart brings. We will never go wrong when we handle others with kindness. Simply remember this and watch as your people skills improve instantly.

Lesson...

Having great people skills is recognizing that every human being has an inward longing to be treated in a kind manner.

Quality #6

Healthier relationships result when we show …

Calmness

Calmness makes others feel secure.

When we show a calm disposition toward another person, we are conveying that we feel comfortable around him or her. Being composed also allows others to feel relaxed. It is as if showing a tranquil temperament makes it easier for people to unwind and feel more peaceful in our presence.

In order to bring out the best in others, we need to keep as much stress out of our life as possible. When we are allowing anxiety and worry to clutter our mind, it then becomes difficult to focus our attention on others. The reason is that worry makes us become too absorbed in ourselves and less aware of the needs of others.

If we are to develop a calm nature, we need to avoid worry at all costs. By becoming anxiety-free, we are then liberated to become more aware of others and their needs. When we do this, those around us will feel more comfortable. Not only will this give us a calmer disposition, but it will also allow others to relax and be more at ease in our presence.

Lesson...

The biggest enemy of having a calm disposition is anxiety. Learn to avoid worry and be set free from becoming self-absorbed.

Quality #7

Healthier relationships result when we show ...

Caring

Caring brings out the best in others.

People will always become their best when they know that someone cares about them. There is no other virtue that can change a person quite like when he or she recognizes that another person is genuinely concerned. This character trait will enhance every other good quality that a person can possess.

When we care about others, it also allows us to show the best in ourselves. Our attitude and disposition begins to change for the better when we care about people. Each one of us can recognize when someone cares. We see it in the way we are treated.

Developing better people skills will automatically happen when we have the quality of caring. In order for it to be genuine, this virtue must start from the inside. *It must be an inner quality that expresses itself in how we treat people.* By cultivating this attitude, we will soon be helping others to care as well. And in the end, the simple act of making others care will bring out their best.

Lesson...

When we care about people, we bring out the best in them.

Quality #8

Healthier relationships result when we show ...

Cheerfulness

Cheerfulness makes others more optimistic.

We often remember when we have encountered a person with a cheerful disposition. Not only did it awaken us, *but it also had the tendency to make us feel cheerful as well.* Having good people skills is about being able to create an atmosphere of optimism. It is drawing out the positive features in others and helping them to be more optimistic in the process.

Showing cheerfulness can be defined as a virtue that sees life from a more positive point of view. It is seeing the goodness in situations and meditating on things that are of quality. It is being a person who sees the best in others. When we have this type of attitude, we then begin to live a more cheerful life.

If we are to have healthier relationships, we need to look at life with a more joyful frame of mind. *By being aware of what we meditate on, we will begin to catch ourselves when our thoughts begin to become cloudy.* Start by seeing the goodness in life and the blessings that are given each day. When we do this, we will find ourselves becoming more cheerful and better at building relationships.

Lesson...

Being cheerful is a result of what we choose to meditate on. See the goodness in life and watch as your relationships improve.

21

Quality #9

Healthier relationships result when we show …

Compassion

Compassion expresses that we understand.

Developing healthier relationships takes a certain amount of understanding on our part. *It calls for us to show compassion when we may not fully understand what another person has been through, or what he or she may be feeling at the present moment.* By expressing compassion, we are showing that we accept them where they are at.

There may be moments in each of our lives where we simply need someone to be understanding toward us. We cannot expect people to fully comprehend what we may have gone through. But when a person projects to us a certain measure of compassion, we begin to feel better because someone has taken the time to connect in a way that brings comfort.

Developing great people skills is simply learning to take the time to listen and be there for someone who may be hurting. It is showing compassion and a willingness to offer a listening ear. By doing this, we will not only bring out our best, but will help others in their time of need.

Lesson...

When we show compassion, it allows another person to express their hurts and disappointments without fear.

Quality #10

Healthier relationships result when we show ...

Confidentiality

Confidentiality shows we can be trusted.

When others trust us, they will be inclined to share more openly. The reason for this is that they will be more confident that we will not share with others what was shared to us. This is having the quality of confidentiality. We can be trusted with what another person has confided in us. *In essence, we have gained the confidence that what is shared will stay with us.*

So how do we gain this virtue into our own lives? What steps can we take to convey to others that we are a person who will keep what has been said to ourselves? *The answer is simply to show that we can be trusted by keeping what has been shared in total confidentiality.* It is continuing the habit of never sharing with people what someone else has confided in us. In other words, being a person of discretion is the key in gaining trust from others.

In order for healthy relationships to occur, we must show people that we are discreet with the words that we use. We must also be a person who does not talk negatively about others. When people recognize that we are careful with our words, they in turn will be more willing to confide in us. Healthy relationships are then the result of being this person of confidentiality.

Lesson...

By being careful with the words we use, others will soon recognize that we can be trusted to keep what was shared with us.

Quality #11

Healthier relationships result when we show ...

Consideration

Consideration shows others respect.

People will always show their best when we are considerate. *This is because we are expressing respect to them.* This virtue not only attracts positive responses, but also allows others to show their best in the process.

When we are considerate, we will soon find people becoming like-minded in their behavior toward us. *This is because they have recognized our thoughtful attitude and desire to do the same.* Very rarely will a person be inconsiderate when he or she has been shown kindness. What we will find is that most people will bring out their best when they have been treated with consideration.

We can never be at our best unless we begin to adapt the virtues that convey to others a thoughtful attitude. When we start to treat people with consideration, we will soon discover that they will go out of their way to do the same for us.

Lesson...

Being considerate will bring out the best in others because people always respond well when they have been treated politely.

Quality #12

Healthier relationships result when we show …

Cooperation

Cooperation expresses we are a team player.

When we show ourselves to be cooperative, we are conveying to people that we are a team player. We express that we are willing to work together toward a common goal. By doing this, we are helping to create an atmosphere where collaboration and team work can thrive and bring out the best in everyone involved.

Being a cooperative person is essential for building healthy relationships. *This is because great relationships can only occur when both parties learn to cooperate with each other. The best relationships have a sense of give and take that only occurs when both people are willing to sacrifice always wanting their own way.*

The virtue of cooperation expresses that we are willing to compromise our own wants. It conveys an unselfish attitude. *People will soon take notice of our selflessness and respect the willingness we have in cooperating.* When others see this virtue displayed in our lives, they will also be more prone to work together, and in the process become less self-centered.

Lesson...

Being cooperative brings out the best in others because it displays a great example of living a life that is not self-centered.

Quality #13

Healthier relationships result when we show …

Dependability

Dependability builds trust in a relationship.

Everyone enjoys being around those who are dependable. Not only are they trustworthy, but they can also be relied upon to do what they have said they would do. When others recognize this trait in us, it gives them the confidence that we can be depended upon. *This quality brings out the best in everyone simply because it offers a perfect example of a highly regarded virtue.*

Having excellent people skills means that we project a life of virtue. It is putting an inner quality into action that allows people to trust us. When we are a dependable person who consistently follows through on our commitments, we are showing that we can be trusted.

Words like reliability, consistency, and responsibility come to mind when we show that we can be depended upon. It gives people a great example to follow. *The more dependable we are, the healthier our relationships will turn out to be.*

Lesson...

When we have the virtue of dependability, we are showing others by example that being responsible is the best way to live.

Quality #14

Healthier relationships result when we show ...

Discernment

Discernment guards and protects us.

Having the quality of discernment guards us from entering into relationships that may not be to our best interest. *To be able to recognize when a potential relationship may not be healthy is showing that we have the ability to perceive what is ultimately best for us.* This quality also allows us to choose the friends who will be a positive influence in bringing out our best. This is the benefit of being a discernable person, especially in the area of developing better relationships.

Being a perceptive person simply means that we become astute at reading another person's inner character. *By learning to recognize potential hazards that certain relationships may possibly bring is showing that we have good judgment.* On the other hand, if we have not developed this inner quality, we may become handicapped with our future choices in selecting relationships that are healthy for us.

Having excellent people skills is being able to make a distinction between healthy and unhealthy character traits. It is having the discernment to make the best possible choices in the relationships that we may want to pursue. By being perceptive, our chances for healthier relationships will only improve.

Lesson...

Having the quality of discernment allows us to choose our friends wisely.

Quality #15

Healthier relationships result when we show …

Empathy

Empathy allows others to express themselves.

Have you ever met someone who gave you an immediate sense that they understood you? They somehow made you feel comfortable and more willing to open up. *More than likely you encountered a person who had the virtue of empathy.* He or she provided you with a feeling that they could completely relate with whatever you may have been through. It is almost as if they could feel how you felt.

Giving people the gift of empathy allows them to open up without feeling that they are being judged or condemned. It allows them to share past pains that they may never have shared with anyone else. *This showing of empathy makes people feel accepted. It gives them the confidence that they will not be criticized or condemned.*

If we are to build better relationships, we must learn to be less judgmental and more empathetic. We need to avoid making quick verdicts without truly understanding what a person may have gone through. By becoming more understanding and less condemning, we will soon find people opening up and offering them the opportunity to heal. Be empathetic and you will soon find yourself being used to help others change for the better.

Lesson...

By giving the gift of empathy to others, we are now in a position to help them heal.

Quality #16

Healthier relationships result when we show …

Enthusiasm

Enthusiasm makes us feel more alive.

Enthusiasm has a way of drawing others closer. It makes people wonder what it is that makes us feel so alive. This is one of the featured qualities in children. Watch them and we will soon discover that they are alive with enthusiasm. Their lives are marked with excitement and wonder.

In order to build healthier relationships, we need to rediscover the gift that we call life. It is learning to appreciate the simple things that we often take for granted. When we begin to look through the eyes of enthusiasm, our attitude becomes more alive and energetic. Our people skills also improve because of the excitement that we bring into relationships.

If we are to maintain enthusiasm, it is important to keep ourselves away from becoming bored with life. Not only does boredom make us less attractive, but it also puts a roadblock in building better relationships. By being enthusiastic, we are showing people by our lifestyle that every day is a gift to be treasured. This in turn makes our relationships more alive simply because of the enthusiasm that we bring.

Lesson...

When we live with enthusiasm, we point others toward an appreciation for life.

Quality #17

Healthier relationships result when we show …

Fairness

Fairness shows others that we are just.

When people recognize that we have the virtue of fairness, they in turn trust that we will be reasonable and impartial in the decisions that we make. This also shows that we can be trusted to make the right choices and will be fair in all that we say and do. Having this quality is one of the major building blocks for better relationships.

By maintaining the solid belief in being a just person, we are telling others that we have a strong sense of what is right and what is wrong. *We are essentially conveying that we can be trusted with the judgments that we make from day to day.* Not only will this bring healthier relationships into our lives, but it will also assist in building better people skills because of our innate ability to recognize right from wrong.

Healthy relationships grow when a friendship brings out the best in each other. It is showing fairness and being able to recognize right from wrong. By living with this virtue, we will develop stronger relationships and build a reputation that offers others the confidence that we will be fair in all that we say and do.

Lesson...

By maintaining fairness in all that we do, we are showing others that we can be trusted with the decisions that we may have to make.

Quality #18

Healthier relationships result when we show …

Faithfulness

Faithfulness creates long-lasting friendships.

One of the endearing traits of a long-lasting relationship is faithfulness. Each person has shown to be faithful through thick and thin. *In other words, the relationship has stood the test of time because of a commitment.* This is the secret in maintaining solid relationships.

Having people skills is no different. When others recognize that we are a person who is faithful, they will be more inclined to trust us. *One sure way of becoming a person of faithfulness is to consistently be faithful to our word.* When we say that we are going to do something, others recognize that we will be faithful in fulfilling this promise. Our word alone can be trusted.

One of the key elements of having great people skills is getting others to trust us. This will happen when we hold to our word. It is fulfilling our promises that will convey that we are faithful. *Without this, our relationships will continue to fail because people will eventually learn not to trust us.* Remember that faithfulness is essential for healthy relationships. Be a person who maintains his or her word and you will soon discover better relationships coming into your life.

Lesson...

Be a person of your word and you will soon discover others calling you a faithful friend.

Quality #19

Healthier relationships result when we show …

Flexibility

Flexibility shows an unselfish attitude.

Being a person who is known for excellent people skills can happen when we learn to be flexible with others. *This simply means that we do not always have to have things go our way. In other words, we can be bendable and allow others the right to have things their way.*

Healthy relationships happen when a person learns to become others-centered. It is allowing another person to make a decision or influence the choices being made in the relationship. Without this flexibility, the relationship would become unhealthy because of the one-sidedness that would occur.

If we are to develop excellent people skills, it is essential that we avoid being inflexible with others. When this happens, people will begin to avoid us and inwardly see us as self-centered. But on the other hand, when we show ourselves to be flexible, people will recognize that we are secure enough to give in without always wanting things to go our way. Develop this quality and you will soon discover that healthy relationships are the result of both giving and taking.

Lesson...

Being a flexible person conveys that we are secure enough to not always want things our own way.

Quality #20

Healthier relationships result when we show …

Forgiveness

Forgiveness is essential in relationships.

When we are a forgiving person, we are essentially expressing to others that we recognize our own imperfections. *Being able to easily forgive is a sign that we are aware of our own flaws. In other words, our forgiveness toward another person is in effect telling them that we have the same capacity to make mistakes.*

Those with outstanding people skills have a way of letting things go. *Maybe they recognize the damage that holding resentment and a grudge can bring into a relationship.* These people may also understand that there have been times in their own lives where they needed to be forgiven by another person.

If we are to improve on our people skills and begin to develop healthier relationships, *it is essential that we learn to forgive.* By doing this, we will soon discover people more willing to forgive us. Not only have we extended grace, but we will soon find grace being extended to us in return.

Lesson...

Solid relationships are built when people learn to extend forgiveness to each other. Those who easily forgive recognize their own imperfections.

Quality #21

Healthier relationships result when we show ...

Freedom

Freedom allows others to be who they are.

Healthy relationships result when people are allowed to simply be themselves. Each person is liberated to be who they are without attempting to be someone that they may not be. *The way that this happens is when freedom occurs within the relationship. We give others a feeling of acceptance that they are free to be who they are without having to measure up to a certain standard that we may be trying to impose upon them.*

When we allow people to be who they are, we are more likely to grow healthier relationships. *Our behavior and mannerism is such that we never demand others to be anything less than who they actually are.* When this happens, we are conveying an acceptance by allowing people to be who they are and not what we think they should be.

Having the quality of giving others the freedom to be themselves will always result in better relationships. This is because it puts people at ease without an inner fear of being judged by our self-imposed standard of how they should be. By giving people this freedom to simply be themselves, *we are expressing that we like them just the way that they are.*

Lesson...

Healthier relationships happen when we allow others to be who they are without fear of being judged or measured by our own standards.

Quality #22

Healthier relationships result when we show ...

Friendliness

Friendliness is our first impression.

When people meet each other, the very first measuring tool being used is based on the feeling of friendliness. I like to call it the *friendly factor*. They make their first judgment based primarily on how friendly the other person was to them. This first impression is a major factor in how the relationship will progress in the future.

Developing excellent people skills is having the ability to project to others that we are good-natured. One clear way to do this is by showing ourselves to be friendly. *The foundation for any healthy relationship must begin with this virtue. It is the quality that gives people the green light that we are approachable.* Without this initial impression, it becomes difficult to develop healthy relationships.

Being friendly is nothing more than showing ourselves to be kind and pleasant toward others. It is being accepting and welcoming at the same time. *This is at the heart of great people skills.* It is making people feel comfortable from the start by our friendly disposition. *If we are to have friends, we must always remember to show ourselves to be friendly.*

Lesson...

How friendly we were will be the first impression that others will have of us.

Quality #23

Healthier relationships result when we show ...

Generosity

Generosity reflects our willingness to share.

Being generous is a virtue that expresses our willingness to share with others. This is vital if healthy relationships are to develop in our lives. *The reason for this is because relationships grow from a give and take position.* It is about sharing and freely giving with no reservations.

When we have the quality of generosity, it conveys to others that we are unselfish. We show by our actions that our eyes are not focused on ourselves. Instead of living in a selfish manner, our generosity shows that we are more others-centered. This is one of the key elements in having outstanding people skills.

Relationships will always grow healthier when people become others-centered. Those with great people skills show themselves to be mature enough to recognize that self-centeredness never works in a relationship. If we are to develop healthier relationships and improve in our people skills, we must remember to be generous and willing to focus our attention on the needs of others.

Lesson...

When we are generous, we are taking our eyes off of ourselves and becoming less selfish.

Quality #24

Healthier relationships result when we show …

Gentleness

Gentleness gives others a sense of calmness.

Have you ever been in the presence of a person who projected a gentle disposition? More than likely this made you feel calm and relaxed as well. Being a gentle person gives off a sense of being trustworthy and understanding toward others. It attracts because of the way it allows people to relax in our presence.

Being at peace with oneself is displayed by projecting a gentle attitude. It expresses to others that we are at peace with ourselves. Having this quality also attracts healthy relationships. This is because great relationships obtain a certain level of calmness between the parties. *When we show ourselves to be gentle, we are also telling people that we have inner self-control.*

Improving on our people skills is being able to show others by our easy-going nature that we are at peace with ourselves. It is displaying by our actions that we are void of any internal turmoil. By learning to be gentler, we will not only improve on our relationships with others, but we will also develop better people skills.

Lesson...

Gentleness gives others a sense of calmness and reflects that we have inner self-control.

Quality #25

Healthier relationships result when we show ...

Good Speech

Good Speech shows respect toward others.

It has been said that if you want to learn about others, listen to the words that they use. By paying attention to what is being said, we can find what is on the inside of a person. This is because nothing can reveal a person's character better than his or her words. When we tune in and listen closely, we can be sure that what is on the inside will eventually be revealed by the words coming out.

Good speech is essential if we are to develop healthy relationships and improve on our people skills. *The reason for this is that the use of our words reflects whether or not we are being respectful toward others.* When we are careful in projecting good speech, we not only are displaying a certain amount of self-control, but we are also showing respect to those who are in our presence. *Without a command of our tongue, we are in effect displaying a disrespectful attitude.*

Good speech is learning to avoid gossip and words that are meant to injure another person. *Displaying inappropriate language subconsciously makes people respect us less.* It not only conveys disrespect toward others, but can also make people think less of us because of our unrestrained tongue.

Lesson...

Having great people skills is learning to control the tongue by using words that build and encourage others.

Quality #26

Healthier relationships result when we show ...

Goodwill

Goodwill is the key to people skills.

When we want the best for others, we are essentially showing goodwill toward them. The essence of goodwill is creating an atmosphere of unity where people encourage and bring out the best in each other. *Not only is this quality the foundation for building healthier relationships, but it is also the key for developing outstanding people skills.*

When we have the virtue of goodwill in our own lives, we become a positive force in developing harmony in our relationships. Our kindness and support encourage others to behave in a manner that displays their best qualities. Not only do we assist in bringing out positive attributes, but we will hopefully be an influence in motivating people to show goodwill. This is because kindness always has a tendency to spread.

When we develop better skills with people, one of the first distinctions will be in how others begin to treat us differently. Without realizing it, the goodwill that we have given out has returned back to us.

Lesson...

Excellent people skills are being able to spread goodwill toward those that are around us.

Quality #27
Healthier relationships result when we show ...

Grace

Grace shows that we are non-judgmental.

If there is one quality that wins every time with people, it would be in showing an abundance of grace. *This is because being a graceful person conveys that we are non-judgmental and willing to overlook minor flaws in others.* It is also showing people acceptance without giving the impression that we are judgmental.

Every person needs grace. It is what allows us to grow and become better individuals. *Relationships also mature when there is an abundance of grace being offered by both parties.* Our people skills immediately improve because others quickly take notice of our non-condemning attitude. They cannot help but be attracted to the accepting attitude that we have shown.

The opposite of grace would be to express a disapproving attitude. Our people skills quickly take a turn for the worst when others sense this. Instead of making people feel accepted, we make them feel as though they were being judged. But grace does just the opposite in that it overlooks the minor flaws and accepts people where they are presently at.

Lesson...

Everyone is attracted when they are shown grace. This is because it gives a feeling of acceptance.

Quality #28

Healthier relationships result when we show …

Helpfulness

Helpfulness is lending a hand to another.

When we are helpful to another person, we are showing that we care about them. We convey through our actions that we are concerned. Helpfulness also has a way of making people appreciate our willingness to lend a hand when needed. It brings goodwill and a healthy bond in a relationship.

Being skilled with people is about bringing out their best. It is finding a way to make their lives better. *By being ready to lend a hand, we are in essence telling people that we care about them.* It may be simply being available to listen, or assisting with a job. Whatever the task, our actions are expressing that we care.

Because helping can be displayed in many ways, the important point to understand is that the act itself shows that we care. By being ready to assist at any given moment, we not only build a solid reputation with others, but also develop healthier relationships because of the caring that is reflected by our willingness to lend a hand.

Lesson...

Being helpful conveys to others that we care about them.

Quality #29

Healthier relationships result when we show …

Honesty

Honesty allows others to trust us.

*T*he development of any healthy relationship happens the moment two people begin to trust each other. One of the ways to establish this trust is to be honest in our conduct. Not only will this build an excellent reputation, but it will also help with people skills because of the trust that is given to us.

There are many benefits in living as an honest person. This quality is recognized throughout the world as an admirable character trait. *One of the most important keys to improve with our people skills is to quickly gain another person's trust in us.* In order for this to happen, we must consistently live an honest life.

Those who are best at building healthy relationships understand that trust is a big part in getting along with others. They recognize that living a life of honesty not only brings an inner sense of integrity, but it also provides a solid foundation for healthy relationships to be established.

Lesson...

Every healthy relationship is built upon trust. One sure way to obtain this is to live a life of honesty.

Quality #30

Healthier relationships result when we show ...

Honor

Honor others and improve relationships.

One virtue that consistently shows excellent people skills is when we show honor. It is a quality that instantly brings out the best in others. *This is because every person is receptive when they have been bestowed with a feeling of admiration. It is as if we crave the feeling of being respected.* Show another person a measure of admiration and watch how he or she will instantly light up and begin to stand taller.

Inside every person is an internal desire to be respected. Go anywhere in the world and we will find that all human beings respond positively when they are shown honor. *With this in mind, it would only go to reason that one of the keys for improving our people skills is to show a certain measure of honor and respect to others.*

By learning to show this we will find that people will also begin to respond to us differently. *What essentially takes place is that we are being treated the way that we have treated others.* Our friendships will grow stronger and our people skills will improve because of the way that we have shown admiration toward others. Give people honor and watch as they return the favor.

Lesson...

When we show honor to others, we are essentially telling them that they are valued.

Quality #31

Healthier relationships result when we show ...

Hope

Hope makes others cheer up.

There is something about being in the presence of someone who is full of hope. Their outlook on life makes us feel more optimistic about what may be ahead. There are times in each of our lives where we could use a little more hope now and then. This is where being a hopeful person comes in. Not only are people of hope able to help in projecting a brighter future, but they also have the ability to encourage others along the way.

If we are to succeed in our skills with people, it is vital that we learn to convey a positive outlook on life. This attitude allows us to spread a little more sunshine into the lives of others. This is also important in building healthier relationships. When we live with a hopeful attitude, people will soon become attracted because of our optimistic outlook on life.

No one enjoys being around those who look through the eyes of despair. The reason is that it has a tendency to bring people down. On the other hand, by learning to live with a more optimistic attitude, we will soon find our relationships improving because of the bright and cheery disposition we offer to others.

Lesson...

People are more attracted to a person who is hopeful. They recognize the positive outlook and desire it for themselves.

Quality #32

Healthier relationships result when we show …

Hospitality

Hospitality makes others feel welcomed.

Everyone responds positively when they feel welcomed. This is because it makes them feel included and accepted. Those who are excellent in the area of people skills consistently have the ability to show hospitality. These people also make others feel important because of the way they have shown warmth and friendliness.

Exceptional people skills are having the ability to make others feel welcomed. When a person is received, it makes him or her also feel included. This is exactly what being hospitable does. It gives people the comfort of feeling accepted. Not only is this a key to better relationships, but it also helps in developing outstanding people skills.

If we are to succeed in building healthier relationships, we must make hospitality a part of our daily lives. *By getting into the habit of making those around us feel welcomed, we not only will see our people skills improving, but we will find that others will be more drawn by our welcoming disposition.*

Lesson...

When we show others hospitality, we are in effect telling them that we accept them.

Quality #33
Healthier relationships result when we show ...

Humility

Humility makes relationships more real.

There is something to be said about those who are humble. Not only are their relationships more real, but their modest outlook on life allows people to approach them more easily. *Humility can be looked at as one of the most important attributes in building healthier relationships because of the realness that it brings in the bond between people.*

When we live as a humble person, we are free to simply be ourselves. *Instead of appearing to be someone that we falsely think will impress others, we are liberated to live our lives without putting up a front.* Not only is this vital in building healthier relationships, but it also is a key in getting along with others. *This is because being prideful makes healthy friendships more difficult to obtain.*

In order to capture the virtue of humility, we must recognize that we are no better than the next person. By maintaining this humble attitude, we will start to see people differently. We will also begin to look through the eyes of equality. This alone will do wonders in building excellent people skills.

Lesson...

Humility gives us the freedom to simply be ourselves. It also allows our relationships to be more genuine.

Quality #34

Healthier relationships result when we show ...

Humor

Humor makes others lighten up.

Far too often we fall into the trap of forgetting to laugh. The busyness and daily responsibilities of life somehow make us ignore the importance of enjoying occasional laughter now and then. *Because of the positive benefits that a little humor can do for our lives, it is remarkable how infrequently we indulge in this healthy virtue.*

People who have a healthy sense of humor tend to be best when it comes to the area of people skills. They have a way of making others feel more comfortable. *The reason is because we all are attracted to humor. We recognize the health benefits of wholesome laughter and what it does for our physical well-being.*

Healthy humor improves the moment we stop taking life so serious. Few people enjoy being around those who always tend to be somber. They would rather spend their time with those who are not afraid to burst out with laughter on occasion. If we are to improve in our relationships, we must learn to laugh again and see the humor in everyday life.

Lesson...

Every human being recognizes the benefits of laughter. Begin making humor a daily part of life and your relationships will improve.

Quality #35

Healthier relationships result when we show …

Integrity

Integrity offers others an example.

Healthy relationships are strengthened by the qualities that are contributed by each person. *We enter with certain attributes that not only enhance the relationship, but also assist the other person in growing as well.* One such quality that will consistently help in this regard is the virtue of integrity.

Integrity can be defined as an inner compass that directs our lives toward making the right choices each day. It provides us with direction and wise decision-making. When we have the virtue of integrity within us, others will quickly take notice of our conduct and the way that we have treated them. Our disposition will be such that people will respect our lifestyle and appreciate how we have assisted them in bringing out their best.

In order to improve on our people skills, it is important to live in such a manner that allows others to trust our judgment. By allowing integrity to guide and direct us, we will soon discover that our lives have become a model for others to imitate.

Lesson...

Integrity is an inner quality that allows us to make decisions that are based on what is honest and true.

Quality #36

Healthier relationships result when we show …

Kindness

Kindness draws people closer.

Of all the virtues that a person can acquire, none is as attractive as kindness. Not only does it help others in overcoming a difficulty, but it also provides a sense of comfort to those who have been bestowed with kindness. *To offer this is one of the best gifts that we can give to another person.* It is also a gift that is seldom rejected.

One of the first judgments that a person will make when meeting someone new is how kind they were. This first impression will make all the difference in whether or not we succeed in the area of people skills. *It is difficult to build healthy relationships if we have not shown a certain degree of kindheartedness. It can be looked upon as the key that unlocks the door to better relationships.*

Each one of us is drawn to those who are kind. There is something in all of us that longs for a show of kindness. By beginning to understand the powerful attraction that this virtue can offer, not only will we improve on our people skills, but our relationships will begin to change for the better.

Lesson...

How kind we are is one of the first judgments that others make of us.

Quality #37

Healthier relationships result when we show ...

Listening

Listening is showing respect to others.

Listening is one of the best gifts that we can give to people. Not only are we showing consideration, but we are also conveying an attitude of respect. *Healthy relationships happen when people listen to each other.* This virtue is also a key element if we are to improve in the area of people skills.

Everyone likes to be listened to. This is because it gives them the opportunity to open up and share what is on their mind. *When we give our undivided attention, it shows people that we feel that what they are saying is important.* Our people skills instantly improve because of the respect that is conveyed during the act of listening.

It becomes difficult to maintain a healthy relationship when we have poor listening skills. This is because a relationship cannot flourish without clear communication. When we listen well, not only are we showing others that we possess great communication skills, but we are also showing excellent people skills by the respect conveyed by a listening ear.

Lesson...

Great people skills are a result of great communication skills. Great communicating starts with being a great listener.

Quality #38

Healthier relationships result when we show ...

Love

Love allows people to grow.

Of every quality that a person can obtain, none is as powerful as the virtue of love. *There are no comparisons.* Love not only conquers every obstacle, but also becomes the strongest foundation in a healthy relationship. *This is because love allows people to become all that they were meant to be. Our whole outlook on life changes when we conduct ourselves with an attitude of love.*

The virtue of love can be defined as wanting the best for others. It is also seeing the best in them. With this quality going for us, it becomes clear why our relationships are consistently healthy. The benefits of love far outweigh any other virtue that we can acquire. This quality will also influence and enhance every other virtue.

If we are to be at our best and bring out the best in others, *we must allow love to dominate every relationship.* We must pursue a life of having a genuine love and concern for others. By doing this, we will begin to see our relationships reaching a new and higher level.

Lesson...

Obtaining the virtue of love will not only enhance our relationship with others, but it will also enhance our very lives.

Quality #39
Healthier relationships result when we show ...

Loyalty

Loyalty brings intimacy in a relationship.

Loyalty is one of the best virtues in bringing intimacy into a relationship. This is because closeness can only occur when there is a sense of faithfulness. In other words, when a person believes that there is a certain measure of trust within the relationship, that relationship becomes more intimate. *Without this sense of loyalty, the parties involved will never reach a true intimate level.*

As mentioned, the benefit of being a loyal person is that our personal relationships will develop a higher level of intimacy. Each party will be more inclined to confide in each other without the fear that trust will be broken. Because of this established loyalty, there is a high degree of confidence that the relationship can be trusted.

The way to become a loyal friend is to consistently want the best for others. When people recognize that we have their best interest in mind, they in turn will begin to open up and gain the confidence that we are a trustworthy person. This in turns creates more intimacy within the relationship.

Lesson...

In order to develop more intimacy in our relationship with others, we must show by our actions that we are a loyal person.

Quality #40

Healthier relationships result when we show ...

Manners

Manners show consideration to others.

We can never go wrong when we show manners. Not only does it convey respect, but it also expresses consideration to those that we have been polite to. By being courteous in our everyday communication with people, we are projecting a sense of honor. This will also bring out the best in both us and others.

Having commendable people skills means communicating in such a way that brings goodwill toward others. It is about bringing out the best in people. One sure way of doing this is to show proper manners. When this virtue is shown in our lives, we will also find that others are mutually amiable toward us.   The manners that we give return back to us.

Developing manners in our relationships will improve as we begin to implement simple acts of kindness. By getting into the habit of being thoughtful and speaking cordial words, we can be sure that we are on our way to becoming a more well-mannered person.

Lesson...

If we are to develop healthier relationships, we must consistently be well-mannered in our communication with others.

Quality #41

Healthier relationships result when we show …

Mercy

Mercy freely allows second chances.

Being a person of mercy is attractive because of the forgiveness that it gives to others. Since each of us has made mistakes in the past, we welcome those who genuinely show us mercy. Offering this virtue makes people feel as if they have been given a second chance. *Without feeling rejected and condemned, the very act of showing mercy sets another free.*

In order to develop healthy relationships, we must learn to show mercy more often. Instead of being quick to bring judgment on another person, being merciful overcomes the temptation to condemn whatever mistake may have been made. *This is important if a relationship is to grow because of the imperfections that eventually surface.* By showing mercy, we are in essence overlooking the mishaps that are bound to happen.

People with the virtue of mercy are attractive simply because of their non-judgmental ways. Maybe it is that they recognize the flaws in their own lives. In order to have great people skills, it is vital that we stay far away from being quick to judge others. One sure way of doing this is to be a person who is full of mercy.

Lesson...

By being a merciful person, we will free ourselves from being judgmental toward others.

Quality #42

Healthier relationships result when we show …

Modesty

Modesty conveys a sense of humility.

The virtue of modesty conveys to others a sense of humility. Whether in speech, dress, or behavior, *a modest person is not seeking after attention.* This is one of the best features of modesty. Instead of trying to be noticed, modest people are content with where they are at.

A modest person also projects a certain degree of inner confidence because of the absence of wanting to be the center of attention. This is why modesty assists in building healthier relationships. *Instead of clamoring to be noticed, modesty gives us the freedom to focus our attention on others. It makes our relationships healthier simply because we are now outward focused.* When this happens, others quickly take notice of a lack of self-centeredness in our lives.

The quality of modesty enhances our people skills because it allows us to take our eyes off of ourselves. *As mentioned, it provides us with the freedom to meet the needs of others without clamoring for the spotlight.*

Lesson...

Modesty frees us from seeking after attention. It allows us to see the needs in others.

Quality #43

Healthier relationships result when we show ...

Openness

Openness allows others to know us.

Building healthier relationships is about being able to freely open ourselves up to another person. *It is allowing others to see who we are without fear that they will reject us.* If we are to have better relationships, we must recognize that being open is the first step in building real friendships. *When we do not give ourselves this freedom, others will never come to know who we truly are.*

If we are to improve with our people skills, *we must simply learn to open ourselves up more.* By doing this, we will not only avoid withdrawing, but we will also help others to open up as well. In other words, by opening up, others will become more open with us.

The first step in learning to be more open is to recognize when we are withdrawing. We will be able to identify this when there is a sense that we are not being ourselves. *A good thought to keep in the back of our minds is to remember that we will always be our best when we open up and show others who we really are.*

Lesson...

We will begin to develop healthier relationships by learning to be more open.

Quality #44

Healthier relationships result when we show …

Optimism

Optimism creates positive relationships.

If we are to improve in our relationships with others, we must learn to get into the habit of being optimistic. Living with this virtue will not only improve our people skills, but it will also attract others because of our positive outlook on life. This attraction comes because people are looking for more optimism in their own lives. It is a virtue that will do wonders in how we relate in our everyday communication with others.

Building better relationships begins with the right attitude. *When we live with a positive frame of mind, we see life differently. Instead of being a person who drags people down, our optimistic attitude has a way of building them up.* This is why people enjoy being in the presence of a positive person.

In order to become more optimistic in our lives, *we must begin by avoiding negativism and all forms of complaining.* By being aware when a negative attitude wants to take over, we will be on our way to a more vibrant life filled with healthier relationships.

Lesson...

People would rather be around those who see life in a more positive light. This is why complaining is so detrimental in developing healthy relationships.

Quality #45

Healthier relationships result when we show …

Patience

Patience is a sign of maturity.

There is something about being in the presence of a person who is patient with us. It is a virtue that is welcomed by all. *This is because we see the need for it in our own lives, and are continually confronted with situations that call for patience.* Whether it comes in the form of needing fortitude with another person, or simply waiting for something to arrive, this virtue is constantly being exercised in each of our lives.

Developing great people skills also takes patience. One day we may feel that we have splendid patience with others, and then all of a sudden a new situation arises that begins to test us all over again. But if we are to succeed in our relationships, we must press on in our quest to consistently be patient with people.

The best way to build this virtue into our lives is to learn to endure during these trying times. It is when we are in the midst of having our patience tried that we are actually learning to be more patient. In other words, we learn to be patient during those times when our patience seems to be stretched to the limit. After we have patiently endured, we will soon discover a deeper level in our patience with others.

Lesson...

We become more patient by having our patience tested from time to time.

Quality #46

Healthier relationships result when we show ...

Peacefulness

Peacefulness is welcomed by all.

Every healthy relationship will be marked with a sense of peace. In other words, *there is a certain amount of calmness in relationships that are good for us.* Being a peaceful person only enhances our relationships because it brings with it an atmosphere of tranquility

A person who is peaceful will cultivate better people skills because of the calm disposition that is projected. This is why people are attracted to a person of peace. It allows for a moment of rest in the hustle and bustle of today's fast-paced culture. Having a peaceful nature can be compared to finding an oasis in the middle of a desert. Not only does it bring refreshment, but it also helps others slow down as well.

If we are to build healthier relationships, we must be willing to examine our own lives. By doing periodical checkups every now and then, we may discover that it could be time to slow down and begin living a more peaceful lifestyle.

Lesson...

In every healthy relationship, there is a high level of peacefulness included.

Quality #47

Healthier relationships result when we show …

Prudence

Prudence shows good sense.

When we have the quality of prudence in our lives, we will find ourselves making better decisions. Having this ability to discern will not only help in building healthier relationships, but it will also keep us away from relationships that may not be to our best interest. This is because being prudent allows us to make the best choices each day.

Excellent people skills are about treating people respectfully. It is gaining the insight to know how to get along with others. When we live a sensible lifestyle, we will soon discover our relationships becoming healthier. It is having the quality of prudence that will give us the wisdom to know how to relate with people in a more favorable manner.

Becoming a more prudent person is also having the wisdom to seek out sound counsel and filling our minds with solid advice. *It is learning from those we respect and having the knowledge to choose relationships that will assist us toward a more discreet lifestyle.*

Lesson...

Prudence will allow us to make the right decisions, especially in our relationships.

Quality #48

Healthier relationships result when we show …

Reliability

Reliability shows that we can be counted on.

Trust must be the foundation in every healthy relationship. In order for this to occur, we must consistently be a reliable person. This simply means that we show ourselves to be dependable and responsible. When this occurs, people will then trust us more and be inclined to build a relationship with us.

This also applies to having great people skills. When others recognize that we are reliable, they in turn will be more inclined to put more confidence in us. *What we are telling them by our reliability is that we are a responsible person who can be trusted.*

The virtue of reliability has everything to do with being responsible. Without this, it would be difficult to maintain a healthy relationship. *This is because better relationships can only happen when it is maintained by responsible individuals who can be relied upon.*

Lesson...

When we show ourselves to be reliable, others will be more willing to trust us.

Quality #49

Healthier relationships result when we show …

Respect

Respect conveys that we value others.

Every person responds favorably when they are given respect. This honoring virtue draws people in because it conveys that we value them. *A relationship without respect is not only unhealthy, but it can eventually build bitterness between those involved.* If we are to build healthier relationships, it is important that we consistently show ourselves to be respectable.

Having excellent people skills is no different. *Those who have an ability to communicate well understand the importance of showing respect.* On the other hand, when a person has a difficult time showing respect, he or she will also have a difficult time getting along with others. It is only when we give respect that we will be able to build healthier relationships.

In order to develop this virtue, we must consistently treat people in a kind and considerate manner. This should become a routine with every person that we meet. By simply making a habit of displaying a respectful attitude, we will soon discover that the respect we have given will be returned back to us.

Lesson...

Every person longs to be treated respectfully. With this said, it only goes to reason that we should show respect to everyone that we meet.

Quality #50

Healthier relationships result when we show ...

Righteousness

Righteousness allows others to trust us.

When we think of the word righteousness, we can also envision similar words such as decency, morality, ethics, and justice. It can be thought of as a quality that brings a sense of truthfulness within a relationship. *By being a person who attempts to do what is morally right, we convey to others that we can be trusted. This is what all healthy relationships are built upon.*

When we live with the virtue of righteousness, we are expressing that we believe in certain standards that should be upheld. Our lives become marked with inner decency. We will attempt to do everything within our influence to maintain lives that benefit our community. In other words, these moral principles help in building a better society.

When a person reflects moral integrity, others will take notice and be more inclined to live honorably as well. *Relationships become more grounded because of the ethical standards that govern both parties.* In the end we will find healthier relationships taking place because of the mutual respect that grows from living moral lives.

Lesson...

Showing ourselves to uphold high standards brings about more respectful relationships.

Quality #51

Healthier relationships result when we show ...

Self-Control

Self-Control displays a disciple lifestyle.

Living with self-control is a reflection of having a disciple lifestyle. It conveys to others that our life is governed by a high degree of willpower and inner strength. Having this quality in our daily lives not only allows us to build healthier relationships, but it also attracts like-minded people who also live self-disciplined lives.

Developing excellent people skills is about learning to conduct ourselves in a respectful manner. In order to do this, our personal lives will need to reflect self-control. By maintaining this disciplined lifestyle, we will also find our people skills improving as well.

What we will also discover is that the more self-control we maintain, the better we will be in treating others with kindness and respect. Being self-disciplined brings both inner and outer respect. This then allows us to build healthier relationships because of the respect that we consistently convey to others.

Lesson...

Living a life of self-control allows us to treat others better simply because of the inner respect that we have for ourselves.

Quality #52

Healthier relationships result when we show …

Self - Sacrifice

Self – Sacrifice conveys genuine love.

Relationships that are healthier are marked with a certain degree of self-sacrifice between both parties. *It is noticeable by the unselfishness that is consistently displayed.* By having this virtue of selflessness, we convey to others an unselfish attitude. This is why living with the quality of self-sacrifice draws people toward us.

Of every negative attitude that destroys healthy relationships, none is as damaging as living a life filled with selfishness. This not only affects our people skills, but it also forfeits our chances for better relationships. Instead of wanting the best for the other person, a lifestyle marked with selfishness only cares about oneself.

If we are to improve in our people skills, it is vital that we avoid selfishness altogether. By taking our eyes off of ourselves and focusing on others, we will begin to see our relationships growing healthier because of this unselfish attitude.

Lesson...

Healthy relationships grow as we become less selfish and more focused on the needs of others.

Quality #53

Healthier relationships result when we show ...

Sensitivity

Sensitivity helps to understand others.

Those who tend to be best in the area of people skills have a way of sensing how others may feel at any particular moment. *It is almost as if they can step into the shoes of another and get a sense of what the person may be feeling.* This virtue of sensitivity also allows a person to react in ways that can help in building healthier relationships.

We are at an advantage in relating with others when we are sensitive to their feelings. This is the beauty of developing the virtue of sensitivity. The benefits are tremendous because of the way it allows us to communicate. *Instead of saying something that may put static in a relationship, our sensitivity directs us to communicate in a way that allows us to build bridges.*

Being sensitive is simply learning to sense what another may be thinking. *It is moving outside of our own feelings and then being free to consider what another person may be feeling.* Our people skills will instantly improve because we will begin to treat others in a way that expresses consideration for their feelings.

Lesson...

Having great people skills is having the ability to take the feelings of others into consideration.

Quality #54

Healthier relationships result when we show …

Service

Service shows an unselfish attitude.

When we enjoy serving, we are in effect showing an unselfish attitude. This virtue is attractive in that it expresses that our focus is on others. People quickly take notice when we live an unselfish lifestyle by the service mentality that we display. *It also attracts because others recognize that our lives are marked with the virtue of having a willingness to serve.*

Having a servant's attitude is being aware of others' needs. It is looking beyond ourselves and our own desires and seeking ways to assist people. *We show by our willingness to help that we care.* Instead of looking out for our own needs, we live with the mindset of seeking out ways to serve others.

One of the key components of having great people skills is to look beyond ourselves and see the needs of others. It is being willing to serve without a thought of what is in it for us. In other words, we live with the mindset that moves outside of ourselves and to the needs of those around us.

Lesson...

Serving willingly shows that our focus is on others.

Quality #55

Healthier relationships result when we show …

Silence

Silence allows others to open up.

If we are to grow in our people skills, it is essential that we understand how silence plays a decisive role in our ability to communicate with others. By learning to be silent, we allow true communication to take place. We also improve our relationships because of our ability to listen well.

The virtue of silence attracts because it does not demand attention. When we have allowed ourselves to simply be silent and listen, we are showing great communication skills. But what frequently happens in the course of a conversation is that the parties involved simply wait their turn to speak. Instead of approaching a conversation with the mindset to listen, the majority of time is spent waiting for the other person to finish a sentence so we can get our words out.

If we are to improve in our relationships, we must learn to be silent in the course of a conversation. We must offer the gift of listening and allow others to speak without waiting to interrupt. *If our desire is to always talk, we will soon find people avoiding us because of our constant need to always have to be listened to.*

Lesson...

We show that we have excellent conversational skills when we learn to be silent and simply listen to others.

Quality #56
Healthier relationships result when we show ...

Sincerity

Sincerity makes us more believable.

The virtue of sincerity has many benefits in the process of building healthier relationship. Not only does it allow others to confide in us more often, but it also makes us more believable in what we may have to share. Having the quality of sincerity gives people more confidence in us. This in turns develops better relationships.

Sincerely is a lifestyle that is marked by authenticity and validity. People will take us more serious and believe what we convey. But imagine if our lives were consistently marked with insincerity. It would then be almost impossible to build fulfilling relationships because few would take us serious. Our people skills would also be undermined because nobody would ever know when to believe us.

Healthy relationships must maintain balance. There is a time to laugh, but there is also a time to be sincere. By seeking a healthy balance and showing ourselves to avoid both extremes, our lives will reflect both poise and a healthy equilibrium.

Lesson...

There will be moments in a balanced life where sincerity is called for.

Quality #57

Healthier relationships result when we show …

Support

Support shows our faithfulness.

Healthy relationships are built upon a sense of faithfulness among those involved. Along with trusting each other, being faithful must play a large part if our relationships are to improve. *In order to make this happen, we must consistently be supportive toward others.* This quality also shows that we are trustworthy and want the best for others.

Supporting others is showing them that we are on their side. Our actions convey our sincere desire to hold them up. We are genuinely happy with their successes and only want the best for them. With this type of attitude, it is little wonder why being a supportive person only enhances our ability to build strong relationships. *It is hard to resist when another person only wants the best for our lives.*

If we are to improve on our people skills, we must learn to build others up. This includes supporting them with our words and actions. It is shown by being cheerful when people succeed and faithful throughout the relationship.

Lesson...

We support others by being happy when they succeed and wanting the best for their lives.

Quality #58

Healthier relationships result when we show …

Sympathy

Sympathy conveys our concern.

When we have developed the virtue of sympathy, we will have the ability to express understanding and compassion. It binds relationships together because of the kindness shown. *In other words, by showing sympathy, we are expressing thoughtfulness toward someone who may need it at the moment.*

Excellent people skills are having the ability to understand others. *It is being able to perceive when someone may be going through a difficult time or just needs to be shown compassion.* By having the quality of sympathy, we become more aware of the feelings of others. When we can sense how another person feels or what he or she may be going through, we are in effect showing the virtue of sympathy.

Healthy relationships occur when we show thoughtfulness. It is conveying our concern for what another person may be going through. By having the ability to do this, others will not only appreciate the sympathy that we have extended, but will also respond well when we may need it in our own lives.

Lesson...

Being sympathetic means that we express our concern and understanding toward those who may need it at the moment.

Quality #59

Healthier relationships result when we show …

Tactfulness

Tactfulness is being careful with our words.

One of the most important qualities that we can build into our lives is learning to choose our words carefully. It is having the ability to speak tactfully. *Instead of saying whatever is on our mind, we guard the words that are spoken to others. In essence, we have learned to be tactful with our tongue.*

Healthy relationships are sustained by the words that we use. *When we consistently show good speech toward others, we are showing tactfulness. Being a diplomatic person is having the ability to know what to say and when to say it.* We are aware of the importance of words and how they can either build relationships or damage them.

We can instantly improve on our people skills if we learn to speak words that help in bringing out the best in others. We can also begin to restore and improve relationships by simply learning to use our words more carefully. The words we choose will make all the difference in our ability to build better relationships.

Lesson...

Learning to be tactful with our words will not only help in building better people skills, but also bring healthier relationships.

Quality #60

Healthier relationships result when we show ...

Thankfulness

Thankfulness changes everything.

Those with excellent people skills are not only grateful, but also enjoy expressing gratitude toward others. One way to convey this thankful attitude is by consistently showing our sincere appreciation. By doing this, we will instantly change our relationships as well as transform our outlook on life. *This is because the virtue of thankfulness completely overhauls our entire attitude.*

People know when they are in the presence of a thankful person. Not only do they recognize this positive attribute, but also enjoy when they have been appreciated. *This is one of the main reasons that thankful people are well-liked.* This virtue is such an appealing quality that it is almost impossible not to appreciate a grateful person.

If we are to build better relationships, we must continually learn to count our blessings by avoiding complaining at all costs. Nobody enjoys being in the presence of a complainer. By genuinely living a life of thankfulness, we will not only attract healthier relationships, but we will also live healthier lives.

Lesson...

People are genuinely attracted to those who appreciate life. By being thankful we will attract healthier relationships.

Quality #61
Healthier relationships result when we show …

Trust

Trust is the foundation.

Healthy relationships are built upon trust. Those who are most trustworthy will be able to develop better relationships. Being a person of trust will not only attract like-minded people, but our reputation as a person who can be trusted will bring healthier relationships into our lives.

In order to build excellent people skills, we will need to be a person who is trustworthy. When people have the confidence that we are consistently dependable, not only will they respect us, but they will also be more inclined to show us their best. *By bringing out the best in others, we are in effect communicating great people skills.*

Having the quality of trustworthiness is simply living a life of integrity. It is conducting ourselves in such a way that communicates we can be both trusted and dependable. By being a trustworthy person we will also discover our relationships improving for the better.

Lesson...

Being a trustworthy person is living a life that conveys to others that we can be trusted.

Quality #62

Healthier relationships result when we show ...

Truthfulness

Truthfulness establishes intimacy.

It is only in maintaining truthfulness within a relationship that true intimacy can grow. This is because being a truthful person is the only genuine way to establish closer relationships. *Without being a person that others recognize as being honest, our relationships will always contain invisible barriers. It becomes unattainable to create close relationships if others find us to be untruthful.*

Healthy relationships are the result of being truthful with others. The same can be said about establishing great people skills. By showing ourselves to be honest and sincere in our actions, others will be more inclined to trust us. *The best relationships are founded on being able to establish trust between the parties involved. In order for this to occur we must live a life of truthfulness.*

Developing a reputation as a truthful person takes place when we consistently follow through on our promises. It is having our actions match our words. When others see that we are dependable and maintain an honest lifestyle, we can be sure that healthier relationships will follow.

Lesson...

Intimacy within a relationship will only occur when truthfulness is at the center.

Quality #63

Healthier relationships result when we show …

Understanding

Understanding shows that we care.

There will occasionally be times in each of our lives where the only thing that we may need at the moment is for someone to understand us. When we begin to realize that everyone simply needs to be understood from time to time, not only will we start to show more sensitivity, but our actions will convey that we care. All it takes is to learn to be more understanding toward others.

Those with great people skills tend to be slow to judge and quick to show mercy. What they do best is focus on understanding what a person may have been through or may be going through at any given moment. *Learning to get along with others is being able to put ourselves in another person's shoes and understand what he or she has gone through.* Instead of making a rash judgment, an understanding person has the gift to sense what another may be feeling.

In healthy relationships, being able to connect with how people may be feeling is essential if we are to be more understanding. It is being sensitive to another person's inner feelings and learning to be more perceptive on our part. By becoming more thoughtful, others will appreciate that we are a person who understands.

Lesson...

By learning to understand others better, we will tend to be less judgmental.

Quality #64

Healthier relationships result when we show ...

Wholesomeness

Wholesomeness sees the good in life.

Outstanding people skills occur when we simply desire the best for others. *Our intentions are always for the good of all. When our motives are right and we show goodwill toward people, our lives reflect a sense of wholesomeness.* Others soon recognize that we are a genuine person.

Being a wholesome person is living in a manner that expresses to others that our motives are right. *Our outlook on life directs us toward making correct choices. Others respect our decisions because of the way that they reflect enduring principles.* We will also thrive in our people skills because of our belief that everyone should be treated in a respectful manner.

Living with the quality of wholesomeness allows us to consistently want what is best for others. It permits us to see the goodness in life and show goodwill toward others.

Lesson...

By living with wholesomeness, we are more inclined to see the good in both life and others.

Quality #65

Healthier relationships result when we show …

Wisdom

Wisdom directs our relationships.

As we arrive at our final virtue that will positively enhance relationships, this trait can be said to be the virtue that summaries the previous sixty-four qualities. When we pursue it, our lives will change for the better. The virtue that I am referring to is simply seeking after wisdom.

Everything changes when we learn to walk in wisdom. Developing this virtue gives us the knowledge to make right choices. *When wisdom directs our lives, we understand that how we treat others is the only answer that will unlock better people skills. We understand that it must start with us. This virtue teaches us to treat others in a way that we would like to be treated.*

When we desire to improve in our people skills, we are showing a quality that is directed by wisdom. *When we are seeking to gain more inner virtues, we are indicating that wisdom is guiding us.* Finally, when we recognize that better relationships must start with us, we are showing ourselves to be wise.

Lesson...

We will always know that we are being guided by wisdom when we desire to develop virtues in our own lives.

Part II

Improving On
Our People Skills

Improving On Our People Skills

As we enter into chapter two, our goal is to begin to discover ways to build any virtues that may be lacking in our own lives. By discovering in the first chapter what qualities we have and those that need improving, we can now begin to set personal goals in gaining more virtues in our own lives. *It is important to understand that improvement can only happen when we recognize what may be lacking.*

By writing down a personal, one-sentence goal for each quality, we will be on our way to improving. Remember to make the goal easy and obtainable. Simply take one step at a time...

"Inch by inch, life is a cinch. Yard by yard, life is hard."

Quality #1

Acceptance

Acceptance shows we are non-judgmental.

How to strengthen this virtue…

Accept others for who they are, not what we think they should be. Avoid being judgmental toward others.

In a short sentence, write down a personal goal for improving…

_____

_____

Quality #2

Appreciation

Appreciation makes others feel special.

How to strengthen this virtue…

Consistently show people that you appreciate them. Remember to think of things that you are thankful for.

In a short sentence, write down a personal goal for improving…

_____

_____

Quality #3

Attentiveness

Attentiveness makes others feel important.

How to strengthen this virtue…

Give others your undivided attention during a conversation. Allow people to speak without interrupting.

In a short sentence, write down a personal goal for improving…

Quality #4

Authenticity

Authenticity makes others be more real.

How to strengthen this virtue…

Learn to simply be yourself with others. Remember that no one will be better at being you than yourself.

In a short sentence, write down a personal goal for improving…

Quality #5

Benevolence

Benevolence makes others respond favorable.

How to strengthen this virtue…

Be someone who genuinely wants the best for others. Learn to also notice their best attributes.

In a short sentence, write down a personal goal for improving…

_____

_____

Quality #6

Calmness

Calmness makes others feel secure.

How to strengthen this virtue…

Allow yourself to slow down and relax more. Avoid anxiety and worry at all costs.

In a short sentence, write down a personal goal for improving…

_____

_____

Quality #7

Caring

Caring brings out the best in others.

How to strengthen this virtue…

Genuinely learn to care about people. Show them by your actions that you really care about them.

In a short sentence, write down a personal goal for improving…

_____

_____

Quality #8

Cheerfulness

Cheerfulness makes others more optimistic.

How to strengthen this virtue…

Learn to fill your mind with thoughts that are noble and true. Be a person who dwells on good things.

In a short sentence, write down a personal goal for improving…

_____

_____

Quality #9

Compassion

Compassion expresses that we understand.

How to strengthen this virtue…

Learn to allow yourself to feel what another person may be experiencing at any given moment.

In a short sentence, write down a personal goal for improving…

_____

_____

Quality #10

Confidentiality

Confidentiality shows we can be trusted.

How to strengthen this virtue…

Be discreet with what others may share with you. Be a person who is consistently careful with their words.

In a short sentence, write down a personal goal for improving…

_____

_____

Quality #11

Consideration

Consideration shows others respect.

How to strengthen this virtue…

Get into the habit of always being thoughtful. Treat others the way that you would like to be treated.

In a short sentence, write down a personal goal for improving…

_____

_____

Quality #12

Cooperation

Cooperation expresses we are a team player.

How to strengthen this virtue…

Learn to get along with others. Become a person who supports an environment where teamwork can flourish.

In a short sentence, write down a personal goal for improving…

_____

_____

Quality #13

Dependability

Dependability builds trust in a relationship.

How to strengthen this virtue…

Be a person who follows through by consistently letting your actions match your words.

In a short sentence, write down a personal goal for improving…

_____

_____

Quality #14

Discernment

Discernment guards and protects us.

How to strengthen this virtue…

Learn from people that you respect. Listen to the wise advice from those you admire as good role models.

In a short sentence, write down a personal goal for improving…

_____

_____

Quality #15

Empathy

Empathy allows others to express themselves.

How to strengthen this virtue…

Get into the habit of being a better listener. Learn to feel what another person may be going through.

In a short sentence, write down a personal goal for improving…

_____

_____

Quality #16

Enthusiasm

Enthusiasm makes us feel more alive.

How to strengthen this virtue…

Learn to appreciate life. Recognize that each day is a gift to be treasured. Become thankful in every situation.

In a short sentence, write down a personal goal for improving…

_____

_____

Quality #17

Fairness

Fairness shows others that we are just.

How to strengthen this virtue…

Learn to love justice by recognizing that only in fairness can we live lives of integrity and honesty.

In a short sentence, write down a personal goal for improving…

_____

_____

Quality #18

Faithfulness

Faithfulness creates long-lasting friendships.

How to strengthen this virtue…

Understand that close friendships are the primary result of being a faithful and trustworthy person.

In a short sentence, write down a personal goal for improving…

_____

_____

Quality #19

Flexibility

Flexibility shows an unselfish attitude.

How to strengthen this virtue…

Avoid always wanting things your own way. Learn to give others the choice to make decisions.

In a short sentence, write down a personal goal for improving…

_____

_____

Quality #20

Forgiveness

Forgiveness is essential in relationships.

How to strengthen this virtue…

Recognize how often that you have made mistakes and how many times that you needed forgiveness.

In a short sentence, write down a personal goal for improving…

_____

_____

Quality #21

Freedom

Freedom allows others to be who they are.

How to strengthen this virtue…

Steer clear of ever attempting to force another person to be something other than who they really are.

In a short sentence, write down a personal goal for improving…

_____

_____

Quality #22

Friendliness

Friendliness is our first impression.

How to strengthen this virtue…

Be continually aware that the first judgment a person makes about someone they meet is primary based on how friendly they were.

In a short sentence, write down a personal goal for improving…

_____

_____

Quality #23

Generosity

Generosity reflects our willingness to share.

How to strengthen this virtue…

Look for everyday opportunities to share with others. It can be as simple as showing another person kindness.

In a short sentence, write down a personal goal for improving…

_____

_____

Quality #24

Gentleness

Gentleness gives others a sense of calmness.

How to strengthen this virtue…

Learn to be gentle toward other people. It can be expressed with a mild temperament, or in the way we speak to others.

In a short sentence, write down a personal goal for improving…

_____

_____

Quality #25

Good Speech

Good Speech shows respect toward others.

How to strengthen this virtue…

Get into the habit of thinking before speaking. Offer kind words that build others up. Avoid harsh words that tear down.

In a short sentence, write down a personal goal for improving…

_____

_____

Quality #26

Goodwill

Goodwill is the key to people skills.

How to strengthen this virtue…

View others as fellow human beings who are looking for someone to show kindness and compassion.

In a short sentence, write down a personal goal for improving…

_____

_____

Quality #27

Grace

Grace shows that we are non-judgmental.

How to strengthen this virtue…

Avoid being judgmental toward others. Extend a full measure of grace. Treat others how you desire to be treated.

In a short sentence, write down a personal goal for improving…

_____

_____

Quality #28

Helpfulness

Helpfulness is lending a hand to another.

How to strengthen this virtue…

Look for ways to lend a hand to another person in need. Simply be aware of the many needs around you.

In a short sentence, write down a personal goal for improving…

_____

_____

Quality #29

Honesty

Honesty allows others to trust us.

How to strengthen this virtue…

Be a person who can be trusted because of the honesty that you have shown in your daily life.

In a short sentence, write down a personal goal for improving…

_____

_____

Quality #30

Honor

Honor others and improve relationships.

How to strengthen this virtue…

See every person that you meet as someone who is important and should be given the same respect that you desire.

In a short sentence, write down a personal goal for improving…

_____

_____

Quality #31

Hope

Hope makes others cheer up.

How to strengthen this virtue…

Learn to see life with a more positive outlook. Remember that only in having an optimistic outlook can we be qualified to offer hope.

In a short sentence, write down a personal goal for improving…

Quality #32

Hospitality

Hospitality makes others feel welcomed.

How to strengthen this virtue…

Become a person who extends hospitality by showing acceptance. Be willing to open up your home more often.

In a short sentence, write down a personal goal for improving…

Quality #33

Humility

Humility makes relationships more real.

How to strengthen this virtue…

Avoid becoming prideful. Maintain a humble attitude toward everyone you meet. Live a life of modesty.

In a short sentence, write down a personal goal for improving…

_____

_____

Quality #34

Humor

Humor makes others lighten up.

How to strengthen this virtue…

Get in the habit of making humor a part of everyday life. Avoid the mistake of always taking life so serious.

In a short sentence, write down a personal goal for improving…

_____

_____

Quality #35

Integrity

Integrity offers others an example.

How to strengthen this virtue…

Make sure that what is seen on the outside is the exact duplicate of what is on the inside.

In a short sentence, write down a personal goal for improving…

_____

_____

Quality #36

Kindness

Kindness draws people closer.

How to strengthen this virtue…

Remember how you felt when a person has been kind to you. Be someone who is consistently thoughtful toward others.

In a short sentence, write down a personal goal for improving…

_____

_____

Quality #37

Listening

Listening is showing respect to others.

How to strengthen this virtue…

Get into the habit of learning to listen more than speak. Become the person who listens more in a conversation.

In a short sentence, write down a personal goal for improving…

Quality #38

Love

Love allows people to grow.

How to strengthen this virtue…

Remember that love always sees the best in people. Desire the best for others. Be happy when others succeed.

In a short sentence, write down a personal goal for improving…

People Skills

Quality #39

Loyalty

Loyalty brings intimacy in a relationship.

How to strengthen this virtue…

Become a more trustworthy person by your actions. Learn to be reliable and dependable toward others.

In a short sentence, write down a personal goal for improving…

Quality #40

Manners

Manners show consideration to others.

How to strengthen this virtue…

Get into the habit of being respectable toward others by showing them consideration in both word and deed.

In a short sentence, write down a personal goal for improving…

158

Quality #41

Mercy

Mercy freely allows second chances.

How to strengthen this virtue…

Think of the mercy others have shown to you. Remember that we all need times of forgiveness.

In a short sentence, write down a personal goal for improving…

_____

_____

Quality #42

Modesty

Modesty conveys a sense of humility.

How to strengthen this virtue…

Learn to walk in humility before others. Be a person who consistently focuses on other people.

In a short sentence, write down a personal goal for improving…

_____

_____

Quality #43

Openness

Openness allows others to know us.

How to strengthen this virtue…

Seek out those that you respect. Begin to openly share about yourself with the confidence that they can be trusted.

In a short sentence, write down a personal goal for improving…

Quality #44

Optimism

Optimism creates positive relationships.

How to strengthen this virtue…

Avoid complaining and speaking in a negative manner. See the best in others. Learn to maintain a positive outlook on life.

In a short sentence, write down a personal goal for improving…

Quality #45

Patience

Patience is a sign of maturity.

How to strengthen this virtue…

See times of trying as moments for developing more patience. Remember that we learn patience through these times.

In a short sentence, write down a personal goal for improving…

_____

_____

Quality #46

Peacefulness

Peacefulness is welcomed by all.

How to strengthen this virtue…

Learn to have quiet moments each day where you can relax and meditate on all the good things that life has to offer.

In a short sentence, write down a personal goal for improving…

_____

_____

Quality #47

Prudence

Prudence shows good sense.

How to strengthen this virtue…

Find friends who have good discretion and common sense. Listen intently to them. Remember to ask questions.

In a short sentence, write down a personal goal for improving…

_____

_____

Quality #48

Reliability

Reliability shows that we can be counted on.

How to strengthen this virtue…

Be a person who follows through on commitments and can be depended upon by others.

In a short sentence, write down a personal goal for improving…

_____

_____

Quality #49

Respect

Respect conveys that we value others.

How to strengthen this virtue…

Consistently treat others with high regard and admiration. See the value of each person and treat them with honor.

In a short sentence, write down a personal goal for improving…

_____

_____

Quality #50

Righteousness

Righteousness allows others to trust us.

How to strengthen this virtue…

Be a person who can be counted on to do what is right. Develop a reputation for having sound wisdom.

In a short sentence, write down a personal goal for improving…

_____

_____

Quality #51

Self-Control

Self-Control displays a disciple lifestyle.

How to strengthen this virtue…

Learn to build discipline into every area of your life. Develop the willpower to maintain self-control and moderation.

In a short sentence, write down a personal goal for improving…

Quality #52

Self-Sacrifice

Self – Sacrifice conveys genuine love.

How to strengthen this virtue…

See the value of living to serve others. Become others-centered and discover a new sense of freedom from the trap of selfishness.

In a short sentence, write down a personal goal for improving…

Quality #53

Sensitivity

Sensitivity helps to understand others.

How to strengthen this virtue…

Always consider how others may feel. Learn to see things from another person's perspective.

In a short sentence, write down a personal goal for improving…

_____

_____

Quality #54

Service

Service shows an unselfish attitude.

How to strengthen this virtue…

Look for ways to serve others. Discover the joy found in living a life dedicated to service.

In a short sentence, write down a personal goal for improving…

_____

_____

Quality #55

Silence

Silence allows others to open up.

How to strengthen this virtue…

Allow yourself to be more silent during conversations. Learn to ask questions. Intently listen to what is being said.

In a short sentence, write down a personal goal for improving…

_____

_____

Quality #56

Sincerity

Sincerity makes us more believable.

How to strengthen this virtue…

Have the wisdom to know when to be serious. Understand that there will be moments in life when sincerity is called for.

In a short sentence, write down a personal goal for improving…

_____

_____

Quality #57

Support

Support shows our faithfulness.

How to strengthen this virtue…

Support others by becoming more encouraging. Convey that you are behind them and want the best for their lives.

In a short sentence, write down a personal goal for improving…

_____

_____

Quality #58

Sympathy

Sympathy conveys our concern.

How to strengthen this virtue…

Show more kindness and understanding toward those who may be going through a difficult time in their lives.

In a short sentence, write down a personal goal for improving…

_____

_____

Quality #59

Tactfulness

Tactfulness is being careful with our words.

How to strengthen this virtue…

Keep a close watch with the words that are used. Become sensitive in saying the right words at the right time.

In a short sentence, write down a personal goal for improving…

_____

_____

Quality #60

Thankfulness

Thankfulness changes everything.

How to strengthen this virtue…

Wake up being thankful for the gift of life. Get into the habit of showing others appreciation. Live with constant gratitude.

In a short sentence, write down a personal goal for improving…

_____

_____

Quality #61

Trust

Trust is the foundation.

How to strengthen this virtue…

Show others that you can be trusted by your actions. Develop the reputation of being a trustworthy person.

In a short sentence, write down a personal goal for improving…

_____

_____

Quality #62

Truthfulness

Truthfulness establishes intimacy.

How to strengthen this virtue…

Avoid being untruthful. Remember that relationships become closer when we show ourselves to be honest.

In a short sentence, write down a personal goal for improving…

_____

_____

Quality #63

Understanding

Understanding shows that we care.

How to strengthen this virtue…

Be more understanding toward others by giving them the benefit of the doubt. Learn to be more accepting by being less judgmental.

In a short sentence, write down a personal goal for improving…

Quality #64

Wholesomeness

Wholesomeness sees the good in life.

How to strengthen this virtue…

Avoid areas in life that could possibly compromise integrity. Learn to see the goodness that life has to offer.

In a short sentence, write down a personal goal for improving…

Quality #65

Wisdom

Wisdom directs our relationships.

How to strengthen this virtue…

Fill your mind with virtuous thoughts. Build quality friendships. Learn to pursuit sound advice from those you respect.

In a short sentence, write down a personal goal for improving…

_____

_____

About the Author

Since 1975 Cary has personally served over 100,000 customers. During these years he has observed and learned what truly brings customers back. Cary's zeal to find out what customers want has been his driving passion in building a successful career as a Golf Professional.

After receiving a B.A. at the University of Michigan and an M.A. at Eastern Michigan University, Cary then went on to receive his PGA Membership and become an award-winning Head Professional at various clubs in the Midwest.

Cary's expertise is in the area of customer service. Having authored various books on the subject, Cary has an experienced understanding of how to win the customer and exceed his or her expectations.

Because of his vast experience in providing over 30 years of personal service to a wide variety of clients, Cary is well qualified to coach others in what customers are really looking for when they make contact with a business.

Outside of his enthusiasm for teaching others the real reasons why customers return, Cary enjoys time with his wife Carol and their three children, Sara, Nathan, and Hanna.

Service That Attracts Seminars™

Helping America Serve Better

We offer customer service seminars to fit your needs for understanding why customers return. The insightful workshops are for both management and employees and are intended to build five-star service within your organization.

We offer Keynote Speaking, and on-site *Service That Attracts Seminars*™ that are available for the organization that is looking to improve on customer service. The fun and interactive presentation will motivate each team member to *want to serve customers more effectively.* Along with addressing why customers return, we will also explore *why customers choose not to return.*

If you are looking for a life-changing seminar of insightful applications for your organization, the workshops may be exactly what you are looking for. The positive changes will be felt immediately! More information can be found at:

www.carycavittconsulting.com

Cary's first book, *Service Starts With a Smile* can be purchased at carycavittconsulting.com. In it Cary shares sixty-nine reasons why customers return. The insightful tips are great for those who would like to build a stronger service team and keep customers coming back time and again.

"A must read for anyone in the service industry!"

Customer
Service
Superstars

We will recognize
them by the way they
have made us feel...

Six attitudes that
bring out our best

Friendliness
Enthusiasm
Caring
Respect
Encouraging
Thankfulness

Choosing a better attitude both on and off the job

Cary Cavitt—M.A.
PGA Professional, Author, Speaker and
Founder of Service That Attracts Seminars™

In *Customer Service Superstars*, Cary looks at what he considers to be the six most important attitudes that will influence every aspect of our lives. By understanding and improving on these highly regarded traits, our service as well as our own personal life will begin to change for the better. Visit us at carycavittconsulting.com for more information.

How well are your customers treated?

Five-Star
SERVICE

Chapter 4
What Makes a
Super Team?

Chapter 6
What Attracts
Customers?

Chapter 11
How Do We
Get Better?

Cary Cavitt—M.A.

Author, Speaker, and Founder of
Service That Attracts Seminars™

Five-Star Service focuses on what great service looks like and how to consistently do it. The book is broken down into sixteen questions pertaining to customer service. The answers are simple and to the point and are a great reference and reminder of what it takes to bring about five-star service to our customers.

Customers will decide <u>within</u> five minutes...

Winning the Customer

Understanding the mind of the customer

The
TRUST
Factor

Cary Cavitt—M.A.

Author, Speaker, and Founder of
Service That Attracts Seminars™

In *Winning the Customer,* service expert Cary Cavitt helps us to understand the seventeen needs of the customer. Every customer is measuring how they are being treated. Everything from how happy we are to serve them to making them feel accepted will ultimately determine whether or not they become loyal.

www.ingramcontent.com/pod-product-compliance
Lightning Source LLC
Chambersburg PA
CBHW062201280526
45788CB00001B/390